PRAISE FOR *WAIT*

"With simple, poetic, and honest prose, Cuong Lu offers indelible wisdom for a life well-lived. We learn about the power of the human experience, in all its sorrows and all its joys, through heartfelt stories and beautifully crafted language. A must-read for anyone wanting to cultivate genuine peace in the heart."

—DEVON HASE, author of *How Not to Be a Hot Mess*

"Cuong Lu has written a down-to-earth book that will soothe and inspire. He speaks as a dear friend, someone who has experienced his share of suffering and has come to see the wisdom of hardships as jewels to cherish. He gives us the gift of no-fear in his encouragement to stop, wait, and study the details of our life, for this is the way to joy. Thank you, Cuong Lu."

—SENSEI JUNE RYUSHIN TANOUE, cofounder of Zen Life and Meditation Center, Chicago

"In a time of worldwide trauma, when it seems raging egos are the norm, Cuong Lu steps forward to remind us of eternal truths. He speaks of the ocean of wisdom that is part of us all, that strength, stability, and inspiration come from within. 'In every person, we can see a Buddha, an awakening being,' he writes. This book is a gift: Cuong Lu's generosity and enthusiasm for life is wonderfully infectious, and never has it been better expressed than in *Wait*."

—JOHN OAKES, publisher, *The Evergreen Review*

"Cuong Lu offers a deeply spiritual appeal to refuse to respond to suffering and despair with violence toward ourselves or others. His new book offers simple yet profound insights into the power of waiting and listening as we live with sorrow and pain. His writing invites a reimagining of how we see ourselves and our world and is a gift to those who have been—or soon may be—on the complex journey of grief and trauma."

—REV. MATTHEW CREBBIN, Senior Minister of Newtown Congregational Church, UCC; clergy first responder at Sandy Hook Elementary School

"In *Wait*, Cuong Lu delicately weaves between our external reality and our inner realm, helping us understand how they are interchangeably interwoven—that there is just one universe. He shows that our only mission is to love and that in every moment we have there is an opportunity to exist peacefully. This beautiful book is a keyhole into the important work of understanding the connection between the inner and the outer world."

—SHELLY TYGIELSKI, community organizer, self-care activist, trauma-informed mindfulness teacher, founder of Pandemic of Love

"An impassioned plea for an end to violence and hatred, this book is full of wise suggestions for how to manage our most difficult emotions. Cuong Lu grew up in Vietnam during the war, and his message to those in despair was hard won and is deeply personal. His 'love letter' speaks to us all. Lu writes, 'Suffering is not the problem. The way to free yourself from pain is to feel it.'"

—WES NISKER, author of *Essential Crazy Wisdom* and *Buddha's Nature*

wait

A LOVE LETTER
TO THOSE IN DESPAIR

Cuong Lu

SHAMBHALA

Shambhala Publications, Inc.
4720 Walnut Street
Boulder, Colorado 80301
www.shambhala.com

Cover art: Amanda Weiss
Cover design: Amanda Weiss
Interior design: Lora Zorian

9 8 7 6 5 4 3 2 1

First Edition
Printed in the United States of America

Copyright page continued on page 150

CONTENTS

PART THREE: DEFUSE THE BOMB
IN YOUR HEART

WAIT

PROLOGUE

I grew up in Vietnam. Americans were killing Vietnamese, Vietnamese were killing Americans, and Vietnamese
were killing Vietnamese. The bullets hit *every* Vietnamese
family. No one could escape or think, "Someone else will
be killed, not us."

In 1975, my parents, my big sister, and I were on
a huge ship fleeing Vietnam. It was the end of the war,
and things were tense. As the ship was about to depart, a
bullet that seemed to come out of nowhere hit one of the
passengers in the chest. We never saw who shot him, just
the piercing of his skin, and he died instantly. To this day,
I cannot un-see it. The memory lingers and still disturbs
me. The question *"What is life?"* stays with me. Why do
we humans kill each other?

During the war, one Vietnamese mother was caught
by an American soldier. To him, she was a Viet Cong, and

he had to kill her. She asked him if she could feed her baby one more time. He agreed. She breastfed the baby, and then he killed her. His belief in love died with him that day. Bullets always hit two people, the shooter and the one shot. This is a common story, with many variations. My wife, who grew up in Vietnam, has told me many painful stories about the war that she witnessed or heard from friends and neighbors.

The bullets flying in the world today will hit *every* family if we don't stop the violence—and it's markedly more out of control in the US, where gun control has been next to impossible. This problem is not about hunting for food or recreation or fending off intruders or invaders. This is about assault weapons available to the young, the unstable, and those who harbor racism and many other forms of hatred, as well as arms exported from developed countries to other nations and as fuel for civil wars and insurgencies. Bullets don't have eyes. They hit those the shooter hates, who invariably are people loved by someone else. If hatred impels you to shoot, bullets will inevitably hit your loved ones too, or at least somebody's beloved. We need to cultivate wisdom, kindness, and activism, and not look the other way. We mustn't confuse defending a treasured way of life or being safe at home with the need for assault weapons. Much gun violence takes place in the homes of gun owners. One day, the weapons will be used, accidentally or on purpose, and someone you love will be struck.

There is war in the streets and in schools, synagogues, mosques, and malls. War has no winners. The bullets hit all parties. The same is true of our *inner wars*; no one wins. If your mind is at war with yourself, make peace with your mind. *Don't act out* your hatred on yourself or others. You may hate a race, a religion, even those who bullied or wronged you, and you think hurting them will end your suffering. It won't. If you shoot them—in deed or with words—you always hit yourself and your own loved ones too. You can't shoot only those you hate. The nature of bullets is to hit everyone.

Bullets have no insight. Insight is only possible in you. When you allow yourself to feel the rage and the hatred within, you'll discover the toll that it is taking on you, and on others. This is the birth of insight, and the moment you have insight, you'll drop your weapon and the tides of war will change, starting with the war inside. You'll see that *we need each other, we are each other*. When you see that you are me, we'll both have peace. Peace also does not discriminate. In peace, there is love and understanding. If hatred arises, we can hold it with love and understanding.

The way to win a war is to stop it from within. If you don't, *everyone suffers*. You might feel exhilarated after acting out, but you always bring your wounds back home—to your family, your friends, and yourself. *And* to me. I am your friend. In fact, *I am you*.

You may think you can destroy those you hate with a gun. Or if your anger is deep enough, you don't want to wait to harm anyone in particular. Killing random strangers might seem enough to quell your rage. But violence also destroys the shooter first, then their loved ones. Shooters always suffer along with the dead and wounded. If you shoot, you hit you. You hit and destroy whatever you might have ever loved in this life, whatever matters most.

If you think you don't want to live, you've forgotten what you care about and dread suffering another minute. You feel frustrated, hopeless, and afraid. Please remember —time is always moving, tomorrow can be different. Put the gun down and try living. It can be frightening, but you'll never regret it. Living can be beautiful. We can love each other and help each other. We don't need to destroy. We need to rebuild. It's never too late. The moment the violence stops, peace is possible.

I live in Europe now, and read news of mass shootings, street violence, and wars all around the world. Every day there's another mass shooting. Every sixteen hours, a woman in America is shot and killed by a current or former intimate partner. Suicides account for 60 percent of all gun deaths. Violence on the streets is an everyday reality; too many people are living in war zones with weapons obtainable just outside the door. Every time I hear another story about this, I cry, and it triggers the haunting question: *Why?* Most US teens fear a shooting could happen at their school, and most parents share their concern.

I wrote this book to save lives. If you have the feeling you want to hurt someone, *Stop!* If you want to hurt yourself, *Stop! Wait!* Every life is precious. Don't kill others or yourself with bullets, words, rage, or ignorance. *Defuse the bombs in your heart.* Allow me to help soothe your pain and the fear you feel so strongly. You're angry now, but if you kill yourself or others, you're also killing me. *I am you,* and I'm tired of dying. I want to stop suffering, and I want you to stop suffering. We can stop all the needless killing if we slow down and take the time to understand each other. Even if you have just one more minute to live, you can live it peacefully. You can be the one to turn the tide, to help create a world where people stop killing each other, where love and happiness thrive.

—Cuong Lu

PART ONE

wait

Wait, for now.
Distrust everything, if you have to.
But trust the hours. Haven't they
carried you everywhere, up to now?
Personal events will become interesting again.
Hair will become interesting.
Pain will become interesting.
Buds that open out of season will become
interesting.
Second-hand gloves will become lovely again;
their memories are what give them
the need for other hands. And the desolation
of lovers is the same: that enormous emptiness
carved out of such tiny beings as we are
asks to be filled; the need
for the new love is faithfulness to the old.

    Wait.
Don't go too early.
You're tired. But everyone's tired.
But no one is tired enough.

Only wait a while and listen:
music of hair,
music of pain,
music of looms weaving all their loves again.
Be there to hear it, it will be the only time,
most of all to hear the flute of your whole
existence,
rehearsed by the sorrows, play itself into total
exhaustion.

—GALWAY KINNELL

My Dear Friends

Seeing so many school, mall, church, synagogue, and mosque shootings; gang killings in the streets, bombs and drones and IEDs in war zones; seeing a man shot dead on a ship leaving Vietnam when I was eleven years old; seeing the world's climate out of control because of greed, hatred, and delusion—it's all so pointless! I know we can do better.

When I was eight years old, my parents had no time for me, and I was unbearably lonely. More than once I didn't want to live another minute. I thought it was a death wish, but really it was a wish for love. I just wanted to be seen and heard. I was sure no one loved me—and the pain was unbearable. I've been looking for answers since, and I've been looking for myself too. Now I'm a meditation teacher, and I sit with people who've hit rock bottom. Some feel they want to die; they don't want to suffer anymore. I've been there, and I can taste their wish for annihilation. Just being with them, I feel an outpouring of love.

And now you and I have found each other, and it's beautiful to discover that we are the same; in fact we're identical. We don't need to be afraid to suffer. Suffering is a part of life. We need to learn to be vulnerable, to tolerate not being armored. We have each other for support. I'm writing this love letter to you to share with you a journey to peace.

Do you want to put an end to the dark thoughts racing through your mind, the pressures you feel every day, the many ways you don't feel seen or heard? What do you really want? What do you really want to end? Your thoughts bombarding you 24/7? Your loneliness? Your despair? What do you think happens when life ends? Do you think you won't feel anything, that you won't suffer anymore?

As Galway Kinnell writes in the opening verse, instead of acting on these impulses—stop, wait, and study the details of your life: the skin on your hands, the despair in your throat, the searing currents running through your veins. Study these things as if your life depended on it. When you stay fully present with your feelings, your sensations, and the world around you, even when it seems dark and cold, joy will arise. Joy and suffering are two sides of the same coin.

The way to free yourself from pain is to *feel it*, not to run away, as difficult as that may be. Be a mountain *and* be porous at the same time. Become interested in yourself, your thoughts, your emotions, your sensations. This might not make sense now, but it will. Can you feel me sitting close to you, wanting to understand your suffering, wanting us both to live fully and understand the truth that flows incessantly beneath the suffering?

Suffering Is Not the Problem

We can't always be happy. Loneliness, despair, pain, and suffering are parts of life. Sometimes we need to cry for help, to call out for attention. It's not the pain that makes us think about ending life; it's the loneliness, the feeling that no one understands or cares. If you can share your suffering with another—almost anyone—you'll feel some release. You might need to look far and wide to find someone you can trust, but there's always somebody. Don't give up.

Here's another insight that might surprise you. Pain and suffering make life beautiful. This might be hard to believe while you're suffering, but the lessons you can learn from hardships are jewels to cherish. If you're suffering, it means you have a heart. Suffering is evidence of your capacity to love, and only those who understand suffering can understand life and help others.

The world needs your suffering, your courage, and your strength. Don't try to kill your pain. Share it with another, communicate it. If the first person you talk to isn't the right one, find someone else. Somebody somewhere wants to listen to your pain, to connect with you and understand you. When you find them, when you lighten your burden and discover the jewels and joy that are alive beneath the pain, later you'll be present for others who are suffering.

We suffer and we love, but we cannot die. Death is not the end of life. Life and death *inter-are*. Whether we believe in an afterlife or in nothing at all after life, death is never real. Look at your life deeply—your history and your future. See the afterlife and the "before life" right in the present moment. Life flows from *before* through *now* into the *future*. Birth and death are the same river.

Do you believe that after death, there's a place where there is only light (or only darkness)? Where there is light, there is darkness. Where there is day, there is night. If you really want to die, you need to *learn to live fully*, with all of life's ups and downs, trials and rewards, joys and pain. They're all part of the picture.

When my son began to ride a bicycle, I'd run after him every time he fell. I meant to comfort him, but he just stood up and got back on the bike. Learning to live includes falling down and standing up. When you're ready, no obstacle is too big. When life is easy, we might not learn anything. In times of darkness, we need to bring our resources forward.

When we understand the nature of life, we see its fragility, and we also see its beauty and wholeness. Some days, the ocean's surface is tranquil. Other days, when the surf is up, we see sets of individual waves, sometimes big ones, sometimes small. In either case, it's all a vast body of water that is made of many of the same compounds as the blood coursing through our veins. Our body-mind is a place where thoughts and emotions pass, and it's also a place with a boundless capacity for love.

Have the people you've loved betrayed you? Are you angry at them and refuse to trust anyone anymore? That's fine. Look deeply at your mind and see what else is going on. The moment we understand our mind, we become filled with love and forgiveness, free of blame, and even of the concept of death.

We think we're born and are going to die, but that's an illusion. I was thirteen when my father died. I thought he'd disappeared, but he didn't. My father is still here.

When I look deeply, I can see him in my consciousness, in my life today. We human beings are magnificent. We cannot die or even disappear.

No Beginning, No End

To live fully, we need others. We need someone to love and someone to miss. Even when our beloved is far away, they are still in our heart. When we think of them, we feel warm inside. Love is a profound connection—to others, and to ourselves. In love, we are more than ourselves; we also become the person we love. Love brings us together.

It rips my heart open when I hear about school shootings and other senseless violence. Why would someone harm others? Why would they wish for someone else's death? If you shoot someone, you are destroying life, and although you may not realize it, you are also killing yourself. In war, mass shootings, suicide, and every kind of violence, *everyone* loses. If you kill yourself, you are killing me too. Please don't kill me. I want to live and I want to love. If we can learn to love ourselves and each other, the whole world wins. To love means to live. Nothing is more beautiful than the flowers and rivers, the ocean and the sky. We are a part of life. Please choose to live. Please choose love.

When we wake up in the morning, the sun rises, and we inhale and exhale, knowing life is there. The birds are singing, the activity of the day is beginning. Are we ready to welcome life? We may think no one loves us, but it's never true. There's always someone. We think no one loves us, but our heart continues to beat. Our lungs breathe. The birds and the sunlight love us. A child's smile is a recognizable sign of love. Love is in you, and it's in the air.

My whole life I've been looking for you. When I felt the most profound suffering, I began looking for something, I didn't know what. Now I've discovered the object of my search—it's you. Finding you, I find myself, and I become the happiest person on earth. I've found life and a way to end violence, hatred, and despair.

What would you like to do today? Would you take a walk with me and discover (or rediscover) the beauty of life? Let's look at the sky and see how deeply blue it is. I was twenty-five when I saw the sky for the first time. I was sitting under an oak tree and I looked up. The sky was vast, and I saw life in its azure and white textures. Embraced by a deep quiet, I fell in love with the sky. "Have you always been there?" I asked, and the spirit of the sky replied, "Yes, I've been calling you, and now, at long last, you hear me. You see me."

How can we not feel the love of life? We're looking for love and don't realize it already surrounds us. We need air, water, and love to survive. Let's walk the path of life together. Beauty is available. Happiness and love are available in every moment, even during the most difficult moments.

Do You Love Me?

D o you love me? Please say yes. Do you love yourself? You are your own beloved. There's nothing more beautiful than you are. *Be love*; be in love with life. Life can be beautiful—give it a try. You are worthy of holding love in your heart. Let's work together to make the world more beautiful. You think I'm a dreamer. Imagine all 7.7 billion people on earth touching love, waking up and *seeing* the sky, seeing each other. Love starts with connecting with ourselves, with our own heart.

Without a dream, nothing is possible. Dreams are the future. Tell me your most beautiful dream. Now write it down and remember it every day. We need to look for our dreams, and when we find them, life becomes a symphony. Your dream comes from the whole of you. Your past includes your dream about the future. Has something painful happened in the past? Is that the reason you don't have a dream? Don't worry, you can dream. Dream that all children will be happy and healthy. Dream that everyone has enough to eat. Dream that we pursue understanding of ourselves and others. Dreams like these can help free us from our past. They soften our pain and make us happy. Your dreams are everyone's dreams.

I grew up in a country of war. I saw people fighting and being killed. I saw very little love, just pain and hatred. When I was twelve, my family left Vietnam and I lived in a refugee camp in Hong Kong. War didn't kill me; I was already dead. I didn't have a dream. I didn't know who I was or what I was looking for. I didn't see a future. I was lost, just trying to survive. My days were empty. Time is only meaningful with a dream.

Now I know that time is life. It contains everything. Each moment is precious. When we dream, we touch future generations. I see myself in the younger generations, and that brings me joy. Young people dream for a sustainable planet and a world that is clean and healthy and free of war and violence.

I celebrate myself, and sing myself,
And what I assume you shall assume,
For every atom belonging to me as good belongs
    to you. ...

The past and present wilt—I have fill'd them, emptied them,
And proceed to fill my next fold of the future.

Listener up there! what have you to confide to me?
Look in my face while I snuff the sidle of evening,
(Talk honestly, no one else hears you, and I stay
     only a minute longer.)

Do I contradict myself?
Very well then I contradict myself,
(I am large, I contain multitudes.)

—WALT WHITMAN, FROM "SONG OF MYSELF"

With a dream, you'll never burn out. You can work for peace without getting tired. When your dream is big enough, you grow large, beyond yourself. The space between us will be bridged by your dream.

When you have your dream, persist. Don't give up. You may encounter difficulties and lose your way. When you fall off the path, stand up. Difficulties make us stronger. People with dreams don't die. Martin Luther King Jr. was murdered, but his dream lives on.

Your beautiful eyes are shining. In your eyes, I see

the beauty of life. In your eyes, I see immortality. Death is not possible when you connect with your heart and the hearts of others.

To Give Is to Live

A single oak tree can have half a million leaves. If we see each leaf as an individual, our vision is too limited. Each leaf is a part of the whole tree. A leaf cannot live alone. It has to hang in there with others.

This is also true of us. We can't be by ourselves alone. We can only be together with everyone. You and I are connected. When you're happy, I'm happy. If you think you're unworthy, that hurts me. The moment you raise the thought of connecting with others, you're already liberated from the idea that you can't.

If you think you have nothing to give, it isn't true. Be generous. No one is too poor to give. Your heart is filled with the wisdom of the ages. It is clear, and capable of joy and gratitude. You are free because you understand suffering. You've suffered, and now you understand how satisfying it is to support others. You've been lonely and you know the value of love. The more you give, the richer you become.

Just as the leaf is on a branch with all the other leaves, when you give, you are a part of your community. And so, when you give, you also receive. You're no longer a single leaf; you become the whole tree; you become all of life. And when you do, you cannot die. When a leaf falls from a tree, it doesn't disappear. It becomes the earth—in fact, the whole cosmos. If someone asks you, "What is the cosmos?" hold up a leaf, or show them your hand. The cosmos is between your fingertips. You think you can die and escape your painful life, but there's no way to escape. However, you can learn to love life.

Even when you feel depleted, burned out, you can still be generous. Text a friend and tell her how important she is for you. Send a small gift to someone you care about. Say hello to a stranger. One way out of burnout is to reach out to someone who needs your help. Supporting others is a way to help yourself. We think work and play are separate. You work hard and feel stressed. But work is also a way to express yourself fully, to give, to be joyful, to love. These are keys that can unlock the prison of your mind. Good work, generosity, simple pleasures, along with time in nature, doing what you love, are ways to break the repetitive thinking and find peace.

Every day is a chance to help. Every task is an opportunity to give. It's not your job that makes you tired, it's *how* you work. Do you work because you have to, or do you use it as an opportunity to express generosity and love?

The more you give, the closer you come to your true self. You're not who you think you are. You feel depressed because you think you're an individual. You are not one leaf, but all the leaves of a tree. Your feelings are not just yours. They're also mine. Your suffering and your happiness are also mine. Your emotions are asking you to look deeply. *Am I an individual?* Giving helps you grow, and it brings you home to yourself. Home is where you feel the love of the whole community. Don't be mad at your parents, your neighbors, your friends, your school. *They are all you.* Thinking they're separate and that you're separate is a concept created by your mind.

Don't hurt your schoolmates, your work colleagues, your family, or your friends, and don't hurt yourself. When you have the idea of harming others or yourself, you miss all the love that's flowing your way. Violence arises from despair. You may hate your classmates, especially the ones who mock or reject you, and you turn the hatred toward yourself. But you are an integral part of the community. We are all in this together. Accept the gift of happiness from me, and from life, and then pay it forward to others.

When you do, everything will change. The cloud will lift. When your heart is filled with generosity, you'll understand why you are here, why you're alive. This is a huge question that can only be answered when your mind is clear and your heart is steady. *Wait!* Wait until you feel like yourself again, not someone's idea of how you're supposed to be, how you're not good enough. You *are* good enough. You're perfect!

PART TWO

Listen

You have to be careful telling things.
Some ears are tunnels.
Your words will go in and get lost in the dark.
Some ears are flat pans like the miners used
looking for gold.
What you say will be washed out with the stones.

You look a long time till you find the right ears.
Till then, there are birds and lamps to be spoken to,
a patient cloth rubbing shine in circles,
and the slow, gradually growing possibility
that when you find such ears,
they already know.

—NAOMI SHIHAB NYE, "You Have to Be Careful,"
from *Words Under the Words*

Everything Is New

When you walk into a room and think it's the same room you were in last week, you're not perceiving correctly. You've never seen this room before. It's different from the one you were in last week. If you see me and think I'm the person I was last week, you're not seeing me either. I'm not the same. There's no repetition in life. If you're truly present and really experiencing something, you'll recognize that it's new, different from anything you've seen or heard before. If it feels the same, it's not real. It's a replica of something you experienced earlier, a product of your mind, not reality.

If you have a beautiful photo you want to archive, you can scan it and save it on your computer or you can print a copy. Consciousness functions the same way. It photocopies experiences, and then the next time you encounter something similar, it shows you the copy and you think your earlier experience is happening again. But it's a copy, not the original. Reality has changed—*it's always changing*—and we're living in a photocopy.

The same is true of suffering. If our suffering repeats, if our trauma is triggered again and again, it's a copy, not the original. Often our pain isn't even ours; it's our father's or mother's or the pain of an ancestor. Sometimes it's the anguish of our child, our spouse, or our friend. When we realize this, we can stop punishing ourselves—and others—and start to love ourselves and others, because only love will help us transform suffering. Love brings relief, like cold water over burning skin.

Sometimes people who cherish each other punish one another for what was done to them. The moment you discover this, you'll feel their pain and stop blaming *them* for what *you* experienced in the past. We humans are not mean-spirited by nature. We're only mean out of ignorance. We don't realize that our actions are based on replicas of reality, that the original event and original perpetrator are gone. There's only an image of them in our consciousness. Our rage can be triggered by a photocopy.

Witnessing

True listening is free of judgment. If someone says, "I did such-and-such and it was *bad*," if we agree with them, we weren't listening. We need to ask, "Really?" to encourage both of us to look again. If the other person says, "It was *good*," we also need to ask, "Really?" When we inquire in this way, we'll turn to our own heart for answers.

If you tell me that you and your partner don't love each other anymore and I nod in agreement, I'm not listening. I'm just a recording device repeating what you said, and I need to listen again. Listening is *witnessing*, not judging. When we prejudge, we suffer. Our life becomes a self-referential loop and we're unable to pay attention to anyone or anything else. We can't see or hear what is really happening. Deep listening has no bias. The listener is free and able to hear whatever is being said. They don't reinforce others' beliefs or impose their own. If we just repeat another's words, we strengthen their beliefs without considering if they're true, whether they reflect something actually happening now. There is neither freedom nor kindness in perpetuating delusion.

Listening is more than hearing. Deep listening frees us from an unexamined life. Our words usually come from concepts—images we have about the world and ourselves. When someone really listens to us, it shines light *beneath* the words and frees us from our notions. Being listened to penetrates our heart and resets our perspective. It isn't a matter of time. Listening for an hour might not be enough, while listening deeply for a moment, free of concepts, can be life-changing. In exchanges like that, both parties are awakened.

Suppose your beloved says she doesn't love you anymore. If you listen only on the surface, you think she's had enough of you and wants to leave. Of course, that makes you sad. But if you listen deeply, with all your heart, you might hear something else—that she's suffering and her needs are not being met, perhaps her needs for attention and connection. Rather than feeling hurt or attacked and storming off, you can try harder to be deeply present at such a critical moment. If you do, you might uncover truths that neither of you realized.

It hurts when she says she doesn't love you, because you love her. If you didn't love her, it wouldn't matter. But if she really didn't love you, she wouldn't have shared her honest experience with you. Love is present, but if you're trapped in images and associations—photocopies—you might say the opposite of your deepest truth. You need to look beneath your reactivity to discover the true source of the pain and the possibility of freedom.

If you don't listen in granular detail with a calm presence and a free mind, the outcome can be disastrous. You might say you don't love her, that you never loved her. She hurt you, so you hurt her back. She's mean, so you become meaner. But what if she isn't being mean? What if by sharing her feeling that she no longer loves you, she's actually taking you more deeply into her trust, enough to ask for your full attention and to *feel* her suffering. If you do this rather than exacerbate the pain, if you listen with love, you won't say, "I never loved you," which isn't true. Your heart will be touched and you'll able to feel her heart. That is the only way relieve her pain, and yours.

Triggered

What we hear with our ear-awareness is an *image.* Ear-awareness, like all sensory awareness, brings forth a perception and evokes an association. We think we hear the truth, but we really hear an overlay on the truth from the past. We hear a drum and think it's gunfire. We get triggered. What we think we hear translates into a perception triggered by what we heard, but actually based on our personal or cultural history. When what we hear lands on a negative experience we or our ancestors had, we are likely to act on past events as though they were present. The failure to distinguish between associations and reality can destroy friendships, end marriages, and lead to wars.

We often have pain when earlier experiences are touched and the fortresses we built at the time are penetrated. We were wounded and learned to protect ourselves, perhaps by dissociating from our feelings. How can we tell the difference between what's happening now and reliving a past experience? Breathe mindfully, stay calm, and *witness*. Stay with the fear and the pain to the extent you can. This is the Buddha's first noble truth, *being with suffering*.

If you sit with your spine upright, there's more space in your chest to breathe easily. Breathe in and out consciously, and come back to yourself, finding your stability. Sitting straight like this, you can listen to yourself and others for hours without losing your sovereignty. You can distinguish what's happening now from what happened in the past—to you and perhaps to your ancestors who are inviting you to transform the family trauma.

Maybe you're a parent whose father beat you, and now your son is having a hard time. What was triggered is painful, but whose pain would it be? Would it be yours? If you go deeply, you may discover that the pain in you is really your father's pain—and his father's pain—and you could stay present with it as it is. Awareness of images that arise, sounds that repeat themselves within and without, can help us touch reality.

Continue to breathe mindfully. Even if someone yells at you or the voice inside you screams, you won't have to flee. You can stay steady, hearing what's beneath the words and distinguishing what is yours from what belongs to others. Listening with love means hearing others—their joys and their sorrows. Truth can be heard only when we're free of rote listening. It takes practice to be free this way; otherwise we fall victim to our pride and prejudices. Others' suffering and our suffering are both deeper than ear-awareness.

Quarreling can be an entry to communication. Conflict can provide a pathway to connection. You want to understand the truth. Your beloved says something that sounds mean-spirited, and you try to hear what is being said and what's beneath that. It's important to ask, "When you say X, I also hear Y. Is that true?" With stability, patience, and honest communication, you have a chance to touch what's essential, which is the other person's pain and suffering. If you don't react too quickly, you might both discover what's real.

To alleviate suffering, we need to be stable and quiet enough to see and feel the pain in ourselves and others. Each of us expresses pain uniquely. If you love someone, you can hold the space for them to be with their pain. Love includes the ability to be present with pain rather than exacerbate it or fix it or try to make it go away.

Mind Only

There is a school of Buddhism called "Mind Only" that says the world and even our bodies are products of our mind. Our mind produces everything—good and bad, right and wrong, problems and solutions, causes and effects, inside and outside, even our ideas about ourselves and our ideas about life. What we think we know is shaped by previous experiences that are stored in the mind. We perceive life through our eyes, ears, nose, tongue, body, and mind. There is the subject (us) and objects of perception (the world).

But there is another way to experience the world. Lucien Lévy-Bruhl, a French anthropologist, called it *participation mystique,* a connection in which subjects are unable to distinguish themselves from the objects of perception. Beneath dualities, there's a dimension where you and I are not separate, where your suffering is also my suffering and your happiness is my happiness. When we touch this living reality, we know that happiness can be found even in the midst of conflict. We can see that beneath suffering and happiness are deeper truths, and so we aren't afraid of pain.

Faith Is the Foundation
of Love

To have faith in love is to have confidence that you can look deeply. If the photocopies in your memory are driving perception, you know how to research what is yours and what is the other person's. I can have faith in love, even when you speak negatively to me. I'm not attached to awareness through the senses or even the interpretations that arise from thought. Without faith, neither perceptions nor relationships can be stable. When two people make a vow to go through life together, for instance, they promise to be faithful to love. They believe in each other, and when challenges present themselves, grounded faith can endure.

Even though consciousness makes trillions of calculations per second, it reaches conclusions based on preprogrammed experiences. When the photocopies in our brains are irrelevant to what's before us, even when they are the closest possible approximation to reality, they're still false and can "lead us down the garden path" (an old phrase that means to send someone misleading signals). It's nice to be smart, but misperceptions sometimes prevail, and in those moments, faith has its place. Without deep faith in ourselves and others, we might doubt ourselves or our loved ones, and relationships become unstable. Faith means first, believe in yourself, then believe in other people. Begin by sitting upright, and as soon as you notice your mind wandering, return to your breathing. Don't allow consciousness to be overtaken by thought. Just breathe and *be peace*. Listening deeply requires peace, stability, faith, and trust.

When you love another person, sometimes you don't have to *do* anything. Just listen. Stay in contact with yourself and in your beloved. It feels wonderful. Usually our presence is covered over by distractions. When we tune in to the deepest, most wondrous parts of ourselves and our loved ones, we discover contentedness, even in the midst of suffering.

Freedom from Performing

We all have notions about ourselves. Layers of judgment can filter and distort, preventing us from seeing ourselves or perceiving life clearly. We can call this limited self-concept "ego." Ego advocates what it thinks serves us and resists what it thinks doesn't. It's an automatic mechanism whose intent is to protect us. But it retains imprints of things past and cannot, even at its most acute, see things as they are.

We're often advised to transform negative experiences into positive ones, but that doesn't mean to suppress negative experiences. If we do that, we become rigid, no longer able to hear what is being said or even to be ourselves. When certain thoughts or ideas are deemed unacceptable, we don't like ourselves when we think or say them. So we may turn our backs on the truth and only show the world what is "positive." These performances are false, and we miss communiqués from our soul imploring we pay attention. We miss them when we think some parts of ourselves, and some messages from the divine, are good and some are bad, some are acceptable and some are unacceptable.

The art of listening starts with being free of our self-image. Our self-image won't vanish, but we see it in perspective, as something the soul conjures to protect us from what caused us harm in the past. We have a persona, but we don't identify with it. We know it's like a suit of clothes. When we wear it as armor, long after the danger has ceased, we don't pay attention to our own inner voice or hear the essence conveyed by the voices of others.

After an organizational meeting I attended, I told the facilitator, "Everyone was promoting themselves; they weren't listening to each other." Fortunately, he understood and agreed. We need to free ourselves from self-serving postures and be aware of the difference between our genuine interests and our expressions (defenses) of our woundedness. When we're free of performing, we have the spaciousness in us to see and hear others.

If we're caught by what we think are "our interests," we can't listen. We think only about ourselves. To listen means to be deeply present, aware of our heart-center and without an agenda. When we already know what's right and what's wrong, we have no room for others, or even for ourselves.

Listening with Love

I f you tell someone what to do, they might feel micro-managed, or even suffocated. A good teacher inspires others to make discoveries for themselves. Refraining from imposing judgments can be difficult. We see things as good or bad, but our perceptions can be askew. It's critical that we distinguish between our resonant, inner self and our idealized image. Freedom from identifying with our image is at the foundation of mindful listening.

When this distinction is understood, our world will change. Countries will no longer make decisions based on "self-interest" (as though our self-interest can be separated from the interests of others) but will instead support all communities and the earth. Rather than conquer and control, they'll recognize the value of collaboration.

A photo of New York taken a hundred years ago is different from one taken today, and neither is the real city. Both are mere representations. You, too, are different from yesterday, and so is everyone and everything. Unless you see your loved ones *now*, in the present moment, as they actually are, you won't know happiness. The photo of happiness in your mind is a representation. Happiness is something you have direct access to—without thinking or even knowing. It's more than you think. Trying to find happiness through the filter of ideas prevents real happiness. Knowledge can be an obstacle, if by knowledge we mean fixed views.

Our *idea* of happiness is never real happiness. It's usually someone else's idea that we've adopted uncritically. We're often trapped by ideas and wouldn't know reality if it walked into us. Because of our rigid, unreal idea of happiness, the people we care most about aren't happy. If we stop grasping for happiness, we have a chance to discover real happiness. The elements for happiness are, in fact, already present. We just have to stop chasing images. With this insight, we free ourselves from the prison of our ideas. To be free, we just need to see what's already present.

Respect is critical. If we have a sincere belief in another person, we can listen to them. Listening with faith in ourselves and others affects us both. While listening, stay aware of your ideas of good and bad without being drawn in by this filter, and you'll hear what the other person actually says and see their deepest self.

We hear either through a filter or with respect. Listening through a filter, we hear only what we think benefits us. Listening with respect is possible when we've cleared the mental space to listen. Then we can hear what's being said and also what is left unspoken. Deep listening is a gift. The speaker feels heard, and knows that love is present. The art of listening is listening with love.

Being with Suffering

Believing there's a single cause to what is happening now is a habit. We think our situation has a cause, and we blame or compliment others (or ourselves) for our joy or suffering. "You did this, or that, and that's why I'm like this." As long as we believe our suffering has a cause, we'll continue to suffer.

Belief in a cause of suffering is a survival mechanism. It protects us from experiences we think might harm us by encouraging us to avoid what we think will bring more suffering. We jump away from snakes or from a truck barreling down the highway. This information is stored in our consciousness, and we respond reflexively. The problem is we get it wrong a lot. We see a rope and think it's a snake. Someone might hear a car backfire; a veteran might think they're back in combat, while another person might reexperience the feelings of growing up in a violent household. Believing that suffering will follow these triggers, we miss things of value. The same mechanism that helps us avoid harm can also cause us to avoid happiness. When we run away from perceived dangers, or from our feelings about them, we also avoid joy and pleasure. We need to treat suffering as neutral. Most difficulties are best addressed when we don't run away.

Parents may struggle with their children. In the process, they come to understand their own parents better. Perhaps a man's father passed away at a time their relationship was strained. Now he finds that his child is unhappy with him. The (old) pain is triggered, and the young father lashes out at his child, just as his own father did so many years ago. If he punishes his child in the desperate hope he'll behave in the way his father would have approved, that won't solve anything.

Another way is to *accept* the suffering the child is experiencing *and* the pain he is "causing." When a child says something that hurts his dad, the father can stay present with his own suffering and with his child. Otherwise, blame arises and he'll miss the opportunity to feel his own pain and understand his child's need. When we allow ourselves to feel the pain, we'll understand ourselves, our children, and our parents, perhaps for the first time.

We don't like pain, but pain can be the cost of admission to gain understanding.

Look at suffering in a different way, and become less afraid of it. Being with suffering helps us discover its meaning and purpose. Otherwise, we repeat the same suffering and reinforce our ideas about blame, and that can continue for a lifetime.

Compassion and Connection

The moment that we see our suffering is a moment of enlightenment. The moment we see the suffering of others is a moment of compassion. We can even have compassion for the person we thought was causing our suffering. Feeling our own pain, we can now listen to others and to ourselves. Free of illusion, able to distinguish between images and reality, the idea of "other" disappears.

I grew up in Vietnam in a quiet city along the sea. There was a beautiful beach across the street with miles of white sand. Every morning before dawn, my brother, my sister, and I walked barefoot along the beach, then went swimming, and when the sun rose, we went back home for breakfast. It was a peaceful life. Then came the moment we had to leave. I cried. I missed my teachers, my friends, the tasty Vietnamese sweets, dried squid, mango, and the many kinds of fruit we don't have in Europe, where my family resettled.

Thirteen years after arriving in the Netherlands, when I was twenty-five, I returned to Vietnam, bringing all my indelible images with me. I thought I was returning to my birthplace, but I couldn't find it anywhere. I ate mango, but it wasn't the same. I went swimming in the same place, but it was different. We used to walk across the street to the beach; now there was so much traffic I didn't dare step off the curb. Hard as I tried to bring the photocopies in my consciousness back to life, the reality was different. This was no longer my birthplace. Heraclitus said, "No one ever steps into the same river twice, for it's not the same river and he's not the same person." That was my experience.

Sometimes we feel angry and hurt by others because we won't let in anything new. So the pain we feel with them just repeats. We only hear the past until the end of their days. To discover truth, we sometimes need a second opinion. All of us have blind spots. We might need someone else to remind us that our "experience" is just a photocopy and not reality. We hear sounds, but do we *really* hear? It might be the recording of a birdsong playing in our memory, not the call of the bird on the branch above us right now. It's possible to sit with our loved one and listen without hearing. It's an art to be free of replays and really hear. To be free of living parallel lives—what's actually happening and what our mind filter tells us—we don't have to *do* anything. We can just focus on our breathing and relax into being completely ourselves.

When we focus on our breathing, we see ourselves as we really are. Ideas of who we are supposed to be no longer rule us, and we can sigh with relief. The ego image keeps us trapped in suffering, in search for a particular idea of happiness.

Our true self is not an image. Real happiness includes suffering. It can't exclude aspects of ourselves, even the parts of ourselves we feel ashamed of, based on our family or our society's ideas that we've taken as our own. But truth also embraces all. When we're honest, we see that suffering and happiness are brothers or sisters. They work together. If we see someone suffering, we don't need to exaggerate it or deny it. We only have to stay anchored in ourselves. We don't have to *do* anything to be with ourselves. Doing nothing, we're available to listen without trying to manipulate or achieve a particular outcome. Being ourselves is a brave act.

When we're in pain, it hurts. When we cry, we can just let ourselves cry. We don't need to pretend to be happy. Being present with pain is, itself, a kind of happiness. Just being ourselves, free of the ideas and images of suffering and joy, is real contentedness. Our true self is much richer than we think.

In love, there is pain and there is suffering. Real love can be bitter, not just sweet. When we're in the honeymoon phase of a relationship, we have many sweet moments. We enjoy each other's words, touch, sensuality. We pray it will always be the same, that we will stay together forever. It's sweet, and we want to hold on to it.

My father was a sweet presence. I was his youngest child; my big sister is twenty years older than I am. When I was born, Dad was already fifty, and he died when I was thirteen. I miss him a lot. Suddenly, the man who had stayed with me and protected me was no longer there. From the moment he died, I began searching for him, unconsciously.

My father knew he was sick for two years, even as the doctors misdiagnosed him. But for me as a child, it was incomprehensible. The night after he passed away, I dreamed we got a phone call from the hospital saying it had been a mistake: "He's still alive." I held on to that dream.

Where is my father now? After someone dies, we still love them, and it feels as though they're still there.

A person can disappear, but love does not. I searched for my father for many years. To find him, I had to transcend the boundary between presence and absence. Then I was able to understand he is always with me.

The Vast Blue Ocean

If someone you love says something awful, remember it's just on the surface. If love is real, it includes the bitter and the sweet. Consciousness sees opposites—presence or absence. It doesn't know that my father is now present, only in a different form. Attachment to form is always incomplete. When there's a storm, wild waves appear on the ocean. But below the surface, the ocean remains calm. The level of waves is consciousness. The fathomless blue ocean is wisdom. If you think the raging surf is the whole of reality, you haven't paid attention.

Listening to the person you love, if you perceive only through ear-consciousness, you might start to feel destabilized. Sometimes it's pleasant, sometimes not; sometimes it's sweet, sometimes bitter. Happiness or unhappiness—it doesn't matter. It's only on the level of appearance.

If I use only my consciousness, it hurts when I think I'll never see my father again. I feel guilty about the things I did to hurt him, things I left unsaid. Like many men from Vietnam, my father was more often than not reticent. When my dad was quiet, I did my homework. I thought he'd be pleased, but I see now, he just wanted to be with me, to take care of me. I had no idea at the time.

There is a child being born somewhere at this moment that is also my father, in a new appearance. If you take care of that child, you are also taking care of my father, and yours. Why stay attached to form? A flower is an appearance; its true nature is the earth. When the flower wilts and dies, it no longer has its old form. But if we look using our wisdom, we'll see that the flower is still here.

Searching for my father since I was thirteen, I've sought out wise and stable men (and women) who can inspire me to discover myself. Parents and other mentors forget they carry this archetypal dimension. Together we are co-creating something miraculous. The child who looks up to this heroic figure is both separate and, in some way, also a part of them. At first, the child lacks wisdom, so as a parent or guide, you can use your wisdom to help the child. A child lacks self-confidence. She's stuck in the dimension of the wave—soaring up and crashing down. She doesn't see that she's also the vast blue ocean. This is not only true for children. Any relationship includes these kinds of projections, places we hurt or are unable to access. We can allow a mentor figure to hold this for us until we are ready to reclaim it as our own.

Parents who understand the dimensionality of water can offer that to their children. When my father was alive, I didn't need to worry. He was there to protect and guide me. After he died, I thought he had abandoned me, and I became extremely insecure. Even if your parents are or were not all that supportive, you can always find someone who has your back. Look around—for a teacher at school, a coach, or another person who inspires and guides you— and try to find someone. After my father passed away, I realized all my friends and many generations of ancestors are still with me. If you cannot find someone in your town or city, try to find inspiration in a historic figure, in a book or a movie. Hold close to their protection, and let it help you feel safe and supported.

Young people today are high achievers. They may climb to the top—but still lack basic self-confidence. To help them feel the love and attention they need, you can begin by practicing the art of listening. They will benefit, and you will benefit. Thanks to your wisdom, we all will open to life. Whether we believe it—or not—how we show up affects everyone.

Friendship

To nourish friendship, we need wisdom. If we live without wisdom, sooner or later, friends become enemies. It can't be helped. The more invested you are in *ideas* about each other, the greater the disappointments will be, and you'll both feel betrayed. All of this takes place at the level of the wave. At the level of wave, you and your friend are separated—separated by ideas.

In the ocean's depths, at the level of wisdom, there's no separation and betrayal is impossible. Friendship in the deep blue sea is beyond labels. You simply share your humanity, your essences. When you hear or see suffering, you try to understand and alleviate it, transforming bitter to sweet, absence to presence, hatred to love. You bring joy to others and feel contented. You help your friend as you help yourself. If you don't know the depths of water, if you don't touch your own natural wisdom and dwell in the vast sea, you might feel alone, just a passing wave, and love is impossible. When you see that you are one with water, happiness is there for you and for your friend.

Suppose you meet someone for the first time, and you have prejudgments based on the other's appearance, voice, or any other observation you make. Because the two of you have no personal history, there is a short window of time during which you're open to being wrong. That is wise. Even if the other person says something that sounds "off," you might delay your response. The jury's still out. You might simply ask what they mean.

Now the two of you have known each other for a long time. You're overflowing with ideas and feelings about each other. When one of you says or does something, the other's reaction is almost always based on your shared history. When we have preconceptions, we're less open and therefore less wise. Wisdom is still there, but we have to make an effort to get in touch with it. The more you empty a cup of tea, the more visible the emptiness *that has always been there* becomes. No one can take away your wisdom. You have the ability to allow in valid feedback, to distinguish what's yours from what's the other person's. It's a matter of time, focus, and keeping an open mind.

In a company, you also need wisdom to nourish friendship. A few years ago, I was hired to coach a company, and I told the CEO that every employee needs friendship and has a right to happiness. I suggested that each staff member be encouraged to ask for help whenever they aren't happy. The CEO took my advice, and the company's mission statement now includes that every employee has the right to be happy. Since they integrated the right to happiness into their company's charter, people there feel free to ask for help when they need it. The staff values its happiness and makes every effort to keep the company healthy, including bringing in a profit. For the CEO to do that, he had to be in touch with the deep, still, ocean in himself. When he did, people committed themselves to the collective effort—coming to work on time or even early, taking extra care to contribute to the company effectively—and staff members reported feeling less stress.

A Perfect 10

Thinking always includes reaching. There's no rest. We think night and day to realize a goal or maintain an image. In fact, we cannot *achieve* anything; everything is already here. We can start with the insight that we're already fine and don't need to accomplish anything.

When you realize you're already free, you can be yourself. There's no need to pretend or argue. The war in your consciousness can stop. Someone may think you're stupid; someone else might think you're smart. Either way, your worth remains the same. You are a 10, perfect exactly as you are. Why, then, do you ever have to make an effort? The only effort is noneffort, to be yourself. Imagine raising a child this way. You simply offer confidence: "You're doing well; you can't do anything wrong. Play. Live. Be happy."

If you start out in life with a 10 and nothing can go wrong, any effort to become something outside of yourself is, by definition, misguided. The natural state of being is perfection. When you want to attain a certain status, to make something of your life because you believe you're unworthy, that's where you go wrong. The more you try, the more off course you get. Just listen—to life, to the voice of wisdom, to others—and say, "Yes, it's perfect!"

When you respect yourself as you are, you'll also respect others. And when you respect others, you'll try to understand why they say and do the things they do. Understanding is the opposite of war. If a child doesn't want to eat everything on their plate and spits out some food, a parent doesn't have to respond with an exclamation point, but with question mark. We can recognize the child as perfect, that she is expressing herself. A question mark offers space. "Why are you doing that?" Interest and caring are the motivations for asking.

You're perfect. No one can add anything to you. Allow everyone to be themselves. From the beginning to the end of life, we all get a 10. We can play, live, and listen.

I Hear You

When someone hurts us, we might be inclined to hurt them back or to turn away from them. We think that will help us suffer less. But we can also try staying in the room, making another effort to connect with the other person. This reset can only take place when we connect with ourselves.

There is never just happiness; there is also pain. That's how the nervous system works. When we feel pain, we know there is connection. When someone is paralyzed, neural pathways are severed. The body can try to find workarounds, other ways to connect, in order to move, but the nervous system, at least in specific places, is no longer the conduit. When you sever your connection with others, you also get cut off. You think it will help you stop feeling pain, but you'll discover that you also don't feel pleasure. In fact, you don't feel anything.

I'm not speaking about a hopeless, abusive relationship,

in which you tried but the other person was unwilling to meet you even halfway. Sometimes we have to give up. I am talking about everyday resolvable conflicts. The more we stay connected with others, the more we stay connected with ourselves and have stability.

If you injure a part of your body, Western medicine might recommend surgery to help you feel better. Eastern medicine has a different approach—to reestablish connections by bringing the whole system into balance. As long as there is pain, you know there's still a connection. To be happy, we need connections. The first element for restoring balance and connection is trust that connection is possible, starting with ourselves.

An employer might think she no longer needs you and might even begin looking for someone she feels would be a better match for her or for the company. This notion arises from the lack of connection. She doesn't see that the company's success depends on all its employees. If she sees this, she'll talk to you and try to connect—to understand you and not just replace you. Listening, she can see your challenges, and she can start to help. Doing so, she also helps herself and the company. This applies to any family or group. Contentedness includes pain. Conflict is an opportunity to connect more deeply.

Listening doesn't overlook the pain that's present. Recognition of pain is necessary for trust in the wisdom, love, and compassion of the other person and your relationship. You respect them. You listen deeply to their words and ideas. "I hear you. I hear your suffering." Listening to another person can free you from fear, misunderstanding, and the idea that you want to cut off the relationship. With deep listening, really hearing, connections can be restored.

Turning Arrows into Flowers

When someone tells me they appreciate my writing, I'm glad to receive their words. I acknowledge the connection between us—the one who calls himself a *reader* and the one he sees as a *writer*. In both instances, he is talking about himself. The focus is not about me, but on the connection he feels. A reader is also a writer. When you have faith in a writer, you are describing self-confidence. You may think you trust someone outside yourself, but actually you feel trust and connection within. When you lack self-confidence, you're vulnerable. Like a bird struck by an arrow, you need time to heal, but sometimes the next arrow, and the next, come in a volley.

The night before the Buddha's enlightenment, Mara, the demon of death and rebirth, sent his malcontents to shoot arrows of suspicion, anger, and distrust at the Buddha. As each arrow hit the Buddha, he transformed it into a flower, and soon there was a sea of flowers.

How can we turn arrows into flowers? It takes wisdom to help a flower bloom where an arrow has struck. When you know it's an arrow, that the other person hates you, you see only arrows, not flowers. Perhaps you believe your child hates you, when actually she loves you. Or perhaps you think you hate your partner, then you discover you love him or her very much. You didn't see it, because you were blinded by your hatred. If you stay there, you won't get out.

When your heart is filled with hatred, you're imprisoned. It doesn't have to stay that way. If you don't put the other person in a box, you might see your feeling as, for example, frustration, not hatred. Explore your feeling. Just doing this plants the seed of a flower, and wisdom can grow. When you realize that no one outside of you is shooting arrows, compassion arises toward both parties—you and the person you love.

Living Deeply

The moment you see that your wound is not outside, you're already healed. Not through time but through insight.

If a table is heavy, it might take four or five people to move it. Don't do it alone. Together, you're stronger. We need community, and that takes trust. First, trust yourself—trust in your insight as the foundation of action. Trust includes knowing that arrows that pierce can be transformed into flowers. In the midst of pain, in the middle of battle, know which wounds are self-inflicted. Understand the roots, the causes, of your suffering.

When you are in touch with your own wisdom, you'll see the wisdom in others. True strength can be to do nothing; just be present. The Buddha just sat still, with all his integrity, and the arrows were transformed into flowers. Doing nothing, you can see and hear a lot. Deep silence is a natural state of being. Trusting in the present, we have less fear. When we react from fear or distrust, pain arises. We hurt each other. Don't be afraid. You're already a 10. Knowing that, be calm, clear, and deeply present.

From the depths of silence, you can taste life without fear. Even disease or injury won't hurt you; it's the fear of suffering that hurts. No flower is eternal. Each is born and eventually dies. It sprouts from a seed, produces new seeds that fall to the earth, then the petals wilt and become part of the earth again. In part, impermanence is what makes flowers so beautiful. They display their beautiful shades of red and blue and yellow while blossoming, and then their moment passes. You, too, are blooming. Even in the midst of problems, you're a beautiful flower. This is your moment. When you understand yourself, you'll live and love more deeply.

If there's discontent in a family and the conflict remains unexpressed, that's a cause for concern. Perhaps members of the family are angry at each other, but no one says anything. Someone needs to give voice to the problem. It can be an explosion, or an honest statement. But fear of fighting or being wrong or defeated can make it seem impossible. The fear that things might go wrong blocks our chance of enjoying our beautiful life.

We don't live to be a million years old. When we truly

understand that, at some moment, we will die, we can live fully now. Fearing death makes it hard to live fully. Facing death makes life beautiful. The moment you accept that you're a 10 in this life, knowing that sometimes things are difficult but you've done your best, you can understand and forgive everyone. Then, when there's a conflict in the family, you'll say something. Really, you have nothing to lose. Truth, even unpleasant truth, brings happiness and relief. It doesn't have to be some absolute truth, just *your* truth, the way you see and hear things.

The moment of ceasing to identify with your image and discovering that you're truly free is a cause for celebration. Everything you thought was your enemy, even poison arrows, are now seen without fear. Even in the midst of quarreling, you're free.

Everything Sounds
Like Music

If you try to live in accord with someone's idea of perfection, even your own, you'll fail. Measuring your life
with a yardstick is not life. Life is inevitably different from
what you expected. With wisdom, you'll discover that your
life, including all the difficulties, is already perfect, *as it
is*. You have perfect relationships, including the conflicts
that can help you know yourself better and strengthen
your connections.

Quarrels arise when we try to change others. When
we can be ourselves and allow others to be themselves,
everything is perfect as it is. Suddenly we're free from
having to act like the person we think we're supposed to
be. With wisdom, we simply appreciate each person as
they are, and ourselves as well.

If we think an arrow is merely an arrow, a flower a
flower, an enemy an enemy, and a friend a friend, we're

just following the customs of our culture. The voices in our heads are not ours. If we listen carefully we might be able to discern who is speaking. We thought it was us, but it isn't. When we know that, everything we hear is perfect and enriches our understanding. It can't damage us anymore. If a friend calls us names, we hear that the other person is angry or in pain. If they criticize us, we can try on the feedback and see if it fits. Without feedback, we might never change, and so we can be grateful for the input and our friend's love. And if the feedback doesn't fit, that's fine. It's not ours, it's theirs. We need to look deeply, though; we all have blind spots.

Sun Tzu and the Godfather Michael Corleone both said, in their own ways, "Keep your friends close and your enemies closer." So-called enemies offer us criticism that can wake us up. An enemy sees things a friend might not, because a friend loves us too much. If we can't tolerate enemies, if we refuse to listen to them, we might lose valuable information. Inferior leaders have only "friends," people who tell them what fabulous people they are. Empires fall when no one speaks truth to power.

A Zen master took a leave of absence from his monastery for six months and instructed his senior disciple to assume the role of teacher. When the master returned, he asked his disciple how it had gone. The disciple was very satisfied. He said everyone had been obedient and done exactly what he asked. He described this as "a perfect community." The master inquired about the monk who caused the most difficulty, and the student said he'd sent that monk away and because of that, everything had gone perfectly. "He was an integral part of the community," the master said. "He's the only one of you who dared to confront me."

The student replied that he simply couldn't bear the troublesome monk any longer. "He criticized me constantly and never thought I was good enough." If you lack confidence, you might see things that way. If you are at one with yourself, you hear things in a different way. Everything sounds like music.

Happiness Has No Cause

When we suffer, we needn't panic or feel ashamed. Suffering is an important part of life. Suffering is not the problem; the problem is *fighting* against suffering. Suffering can't cause suffering. Suffering is just suffering. But fighting against suffering can. There are techniques that can help alleviate suffering, but sometimes it's beneficial just to be with our suffering.

There's nothing wrong with crying when you feel pain—whether physical, spiritual, or emotional. If you're hungry, you need to eat. If you're tired, you need to sleep. And if you're suffering, you might need to cry. You don't have to exaggerate your suffering. Without amplifying it, suffering can be satisfying and informative.

Cause and effect inter-are. "Which comes first, the chicken or the egg?" is not a real question. We can't have an egg without a chicken, and we can't have a chicken without an egg.

If you try to obliterate the cause of your suffering, you'll just exacerbate the suffering. The people around us might not be able to bear to see us suffer, but suffering is a natural process. It's important that we understand—and *feel*—our suffering. We're used to seeking happiness outside ourselves, so it's difficult to discover the happiness in our own suffering. But if we don't fight against it, eventually happiness will surface. When we reject suffering, we reject happiness.

Real happiness is stable in good times and bad. It's present when things are going well and also when they're not. It's even there when we suffer. We think that when we suffer, happiness is absent, but that's not true. Happiness is also there when we're in pain. We try to maximize happiness, but real happiness is not something we can strive for. It's already here. True happiness can't be lost. When you sit quietly, you feel it. The main thing that stands between us and happiness is our *idea* of happiness. What we call happiness is limiting. Take a moment and write down your ideas of happiness. For some, it might be web surfing or playing video games. But is that real happiness? What about wine? Are you happy when you have a delicious piece of chocolate? Or a lot of money?

We work day and night to achieve our idea of happiness, so it's important to know what it is. If you're not addicted to surfing the web, video games, wine, or a big bank account, what does make you happy? Maybe you think that to be happy, you need to have a nice feeling. But you can't have pleasant feelings all day long, so that idea needs to be challenged too. What did you write down? What conditions do you think you need to be happy?

True happiness has no cause. *It's already here.* In our usual, dualistic thinking, we divide the world into causes and effects, good and bad, suffering and happiness. These are false dichotomies. Instead of either/or, try both/and. You can be happy in the midst of suffering. Don't take my word for it; see if you can experience this directly. In the heat of suffering, see if you can also experience the coolness of happiness.

PART THREE

Defuse the Bomb
in Your Heart

If I were a bomb
ready to explode,
if I have become
dangerous to your life,
then you must take care of me.
You think you can get away from me,
but how?
I am here, right in your midst.
(You cannot remove me from your life.)
And I may explode
at any time.
I need your care.
I need your time . . .

—Thich Nhat Hanh, "Defuse Me,"
from *Call Me By My True Names*

Coming Home

Many years after leaving Vietnam, I returned with my teacher Thich Nhat Hanh and a group of monastics. Thich Nhat Hanh had been in exile for forty years, and we came home on New Year's Day (Têt). Têt is a day for families to come together and celebrate the birth of something new, a new year, a chance to begin anew. Every mistake is forgiven, and we have a chance to renew our love and live together happily. In that spirit, we went to Vietnam as children coming home to our families after a very long journey. Thich Nhat Hanh was warmly welcomed at the airport by thousands of people. It was deeply moving.

To come home is to return to ourselves. We don't need Google Maps to give us directions. Home is in our heart. If you live with someone and you say, "Honey, I'm home," and they respond, "I'm so glad you're here," you're happy, of course. When they add, "I love you," you're overjoyed. If they give you a kiss, you're ecstatic. But what if they're in a bad mood and ignore you, or what if your words lead to an argument? Are you homeless? It's up to you. If you react, you'll both suffer. If you turn around and head out the door, you'll both suffer. Your happiness was conditional. It relied on someone acting a certain way, and they didn't.

My Suffering Is Mine

Blame is a habit. "My suffering is because of you" is a belief, not a fact. Your loved one may be unkind or they might not say anything, but it's not automatic that you'll suffer. There's never a single cause; there are always multiple factors. Even if they're under stress and exploding, you don't have to suffer. Instead of fighting against their anger, you can be present with it and try to understand. Not being derailed by your loved one's bad day is a sign of love. When you love someone, you can allow them to suffer. You don't have to fix everything. In fact, it might not even be felt as negative, just an expression of energy. Your partner doesn't always have to be nice.

The energy of happiness cannot grow or diminish. It doesn't arrive or depart. The same is true of wisdom. Through the wisdom that is always present in you, you can see things as they are. With wisdom, you can see that greed and addiction engender suffering. No one else made you suffer.

If someone you love speaks in a way that triggers your anger, you might say, "How dare you talk to me like that." But with wisdom, you'll recognize that it's your reaction and not bring them into it. Their speech is their responsibility; your response is yours. When you recognize your own suffering, you can allow them theirs. And when you recognize your own happiness, you can allow them theirs.

Dealing with Anger

As we begin to take responsibility for our own suffering, we feel happy right away. Clarity is there. When we say, "This is my anger, this is my suffering," we feel happy, even within the anger. Even if you feel hatred toward someone, if you realize it's *your* hatred, you're already free. Later, when anger has passed, we don't need to wait; we're already happy. We seek freedom and happiness and don't realize they're already here.

More often than not, we build fortresses to protect our second-rate happiness, and then in a moment of rage, we destroy everything. Rage is a wildfire that burns down forests. Even if you graduate with honors, find meaningful, well-paying work, marry the prince or princess of your dreams, have beautiful children, and attain great success, a single moment of anger can destroy it all. Is anger the cause? Is it society? The state of the world can contribute to our anger, but it's never the cause. Where does anger come from? It comes from a lack of trust. We don't trust our happiness, so we run away from difficulties, get angry, want revenge. Sometimes we lose ourselves in rage. At moments like that, there is no "self," just rage. When we're not drowning in anger, there's also an observer present. We're angry, but we're not subsumed by it. To do that, a kind of self-confidence is needed.

If you don't have confidence in your own wisdom, you can lose yourself in suffering. When you're able to step back and see "This is suffering," it's a moment of awakening. Don't underestimate its importance. Awakening—enlightenment—is to know suffering as suffering, and not try to sugarcoat or deny it. You're angry, and you know "This is suffering." You're not trying to make it smaller, and because of that, you're not going to make it bigger either. In the heat of an explosion, try to accept that anger is present. Try to tolerate it as it is—no more and no less.

The same is true of happiness. Real happiness can't be made larger or smaller. Just enjoy it. You can see happiness as it is and suffering as it is without trying to fix anything. If you try to make anything into something it isn't, the more you do, the worse things will get. Doing nothing—in *the midst of it all*—can bring deep peace. If you want to cool the flames of anger—to defuse the bomb in your heart—the first step is to recognize anger as anger, neither good nor bad. There's no need to suppress or transform it.

To Every Thing,
There Is a Season

In the Book of Ecclesiastes, attributed to King Solomon, the third verse begins: "To every thing there is a season, and a time to every purpose under the heaven: A time to be born, and a time to die; a time to plant, a time to reap that which is planted."

In many traditional cultures, including Vietnam, where my wife and I were born, this is understood. But in the West, when we feel unwell or sad, we panic, as though aging and suffering are not supposed to arise. We equate youth with health and beauty, and we do everything we can to insulate ourselves from discomfort. Aging is treated as a disease, the cure for which is a combination of denial and incessant vitality. Industries from supplements and pharmaceuticals to plastic surgery and yoga pants thrive because we fear sickness, aging, and death. They market illusions, and we buy them.

When my wife had been in Holland for a few years, one day she walked past a mortuary and saw a woman alone, crying alongside a coffin. "In Vietnam," she reminded me, "there'd be a hundred family members consoling her. The extended family would all come together to say goodbye to their beloved elder." For traditional cultures, death is a part of life, and we celebrate "going home" to our ancestors. There's a lot of crying, of course, but there's also a warm feeling; it's a kind of homecoming. My wife was crying, she felt so much pain for that woman's loneliness.

Dying at the end of a ripe, old life is very different from what I'm writing about—preventing the violence that brings harm to so many, mostly young victims. There are seasons for everything, and if you're in the springtime of your life, or even summer or autumn, please live deeply every day to the fullest extent possible. Stay in close touch with yourself, with others, and the world. Know your mind, body, and spirit, and live as happily as you can. Then, when you come to the end of your days, you'll allow winter to take its course, without regret.

Once while my wife was visiting Hong Kong, her grandmother phoned her from Vietnam and asked her to visit. My wife said she couldn't, and her grandma said, "Take care of the children. I'm going to die this afternoon." She said it as though she were going to the supermarket. She had no fear of death, and that afternoon, she died peacefully at the age of ninety-nine. Her life span was complete, and she accepted that her body was ready to let go.

One of my grandmothers did the same thing. It was before I was born. She said to my mom, "I'm going to die this afternoon," and my mother asked, "What time?" Grandma said, "Six o'clock," and Mom said, "Good, I'll take the train and be there with you." They shared a *home*, in the material sense—they actually lived together —and in the deepest sense. They knew who they were, and both had a profound sense of belonging. When you have a home, within and without, you can live and die without fear. You become more than yourself and feel much less lonely; you know you are both yourself *and* your loved ones. My grandmother could never really die. Even today, she is still in our hearts.

There is another tradition in Vietnam in which the elderly purchase a coffin, bring it home, and lie down in it to see if it's a good fit. Traditionally, three or four generations lived together in one house. Nowadays we have facilities for the elderly. Even in the best nursing homes, our grandparents can feel lonely and even useless, as though they have nothing left to give. In fact, the elderly have a lot to offer. They know the value of life, understand forgiveness, and can draw on their wisdom and experience to resolve conflicts. In traditional cultures, the elderly are highly respected, without having to prove anything. Even when they are not *doing* anything, their presence is valued. It's a blessing when our elders have the energy to work at what they love into their eighties or nineties, but they don't have to prove their worth. Just being themselves, ourselves, is enough.

Life

Many of us believe that an "I" is born, lives, and then dies, and we have no idea that this "I" is fabricated by our thinking. We posit an "I" that is continuous, connecting the disparate dots of a life. We speak, we write, we act, and we believe this identity is real, permanent, and substantial. In some fields of inquiry, this "I" is called *ego*. We not only see an ego in ourselves but in everything we think about. An "I" is born at a certain time, continues for one life span, and then it dies.

When we look at anger, we can also see it as an ego with a life span. It is born at a certain time, and then it dies. But if we look more deeply, there is no "I" in anger or in our own life story. So we get angry with anger. Why are you there? Why am I angry? I don't want to be angry. Or why are they mad at me? What have I done wrong? These questions arise from the belief that "I" am angry with "you," or "you" are angry with "I." In either case, there has to be a perpetrator and a victim.

Where were you before you were born? In your father's and mother's DNA? And before that? Where was your mother before she was born? A bit with Grandpa and a bit with Grandma. It goes on and on. The idea that we are one person, with distinct boundaries, and a clear "before" and "after," someone who was born on the date of our "birthday," is naïve. When this belief in an "I" is seen in perspective, suffering stops. We're not just "I." We are multitudes.

My body is also your body; my feelings are your feelings. I can feel your suffering and the suffering of your father. This compassion is the ground of understanding and forgiveness. And compassion is only possible when there's no difference between us. You cannot say this body is an "I." If anything, it's a "we." Our bodies have been born millions of times. This morning, I ate cheese, and so there's a bit of a cow in me. You may think I'm human, but if you look closely, you'll see that I'm a cow, a chicken, and a turkey, not just a person.

You can never grow old. Even if you live to be two hundred years old, you're younger than your ancestors and also younger than your not-yet-born grandchildren.

Look deeply and you'll see your ancestors and also your descendants in you. You are not getting old, and you're not going to die, because there is no singular "you." Your body, mind, and spirit are so much more than the "I" you identify with. Why try to look youthful? You are eternal. Your ancestors, children, and future generations are *in you*. When you know this, you'll realize you will never die.

The clouds of depression, the flames of anger, in you are all based on a misconception. They are about a "me" that doesn't exist: "*I* feel disrespected." "You don't see *me*." "You don't pay attention to *me*." "You don't understand *me*." If you don't get respect, attention, recognition, and validation from the outside, try not to feel depressed or angry. You can never be validated from the outside, only from within. And self-validation can only be there when you know you are an integral part of the cosmos. If you sit with me or with another friend, you will feel our support, and you will know you are part of a vast community of friends and neighbors, family and coworkers, and even enemies and those you don't like at all. We're all in this together.

The Dance of Anger

I f I light a match, fire can come into existence if conditions like fuel and oxygen are present. Without the necessary conditions, the fire will never light. Anger is the same. Anger arises when conditions are favorable, and it stays alive because we fuel it. When conditions are no longer present for fire or anger, we might wonder, "Where is it? Where did it go?" It is *extinguished* for now. But if conditions re-constellate, the fire might burst forth again.

Anger is more than just anger. It contains all the other emotions as well, including happiness. For a moment, the fire was too hot to touch, but now we can touch it safely. When the conditions that came together and produced anger are no longer there, we can reenter the space without burning our fingers. Anger is a fire that's burning. We might think that if we don't do something to intervene, it will burn forever. But nothing lasts forever. It remains only as long as there is fuel. When we stop fueling our anger, it will dissipate and make room for something else to take its place. In fact, coolness was already present, right in the fire.

Joy is also present, and the opposite is true too. In the midst of joy, we can sense anger. In this moment we're kind and friendly, but in a flash, anger can begin to burn. Kindness doesn't last forever either. When you fall in love, you have to know that at some point, you'll get angry and fight with each other. Being angry isn't a bad thing. It's an important step in the dance of intimacy, with ourselves and others. It's only a problem if you think you're never supposed to get angry, or even worse, if you think you're never angry.

In some communities, anger is taboo. Everyone is always smiling and friendly, gentle and kind. At first glance, it might feel like paradise. But if you look more deeply or stay a while, you'll discover that it's actually a hell realm. When we glorify peace and happiness, we might want to eradicate those who disturb our "peace." Every community has a shadow and needs a disruptive force to help shine the light *everywhere*.

When someone is angry, you can thank them for their honest expression. To own your anger requires trust. If you don't trust, you won't reveal your pain or distress.

When two people love each other, they can say, "Thank you for sharing your suffering. Thank you for your trust." Even if it's someone not close to you—a public figure or someone you barely know—you can say to yourself, about the other person, "You're angry, therefore I know you're suffering. I won't say or do anything to fuel your anger further." Taking that stance, you help the other person and you help yourself.

If you're honest and shine light together on the conditions that gave rise to the quarrel, it isn't disruptive. It's honest, and a factor in increasing intimacy. In that kind of quarreling and anger, you'll always find peace and happiness. After an honest exchange, you will stop fueling your anger. It doesn't take long. But if you keep fueling anger, it will keep burning and causing damage.

Which Wolf Will You Feed?

In a story attributed to the Cherokee Nation, an old man is teaching his grandson about life. "There is a fight going on inside me," the elder says to the boy. "It's a battle between two wolves. One is anger, envy, sorrow, regret, greed, arrogance, self-pity, guilt, resentment, inferiority, lies, false pride, superiority, and ego. The other is good and altruistic, generous and kind." The boy asks, "Which one will win, Grandfather?" and the elder says, "The wolf I feed."

It can be difficult to extricate ourselves from anger. We can't control others. But we can stop feeding the wolf of anger. In movies, when the bomb squad comes, it takes only one mindful person, working step-by-step, to dismantle the bomb. We can do the same by feeling our feelings, observing our thoughts, and containing our speech and actions. Acting out feeds anger, no matter how *right* we are. We don't have to be silent to stop feeding anger, but we do need to mind our words, to ourselves and to others. Sometimes, the more we say, the more we fuel anger. Even when we try to communicate *truth*, what we say is just our opinion. It's often best to be still and look deeply. When we can de-escalate a volatile situation by not feeding anger, compassion arises. The two always go together.

Suffering can cover over our happiness. It's not that happiness isn't there, but it's covered. It's like sunshine and clouds. The sun is visible on a beautiful day, but it's also there during a storm. When it's raining, the sky is covered by clouds and we don't see the sunshine, but it's there, behind the clouds.

The Sharing Economy

People have the false idea that the accumulation of money, in itself, will bring them happiness. Our society, through advertising and a culture of acquisitiveness, promulgates this impression—even though in our hearts, we know that isn't true. Some people are driven to earn more and more, even when they already have enough. Does *anyone* need to be a billionaire? We need to ask ourselves, When is enough, enough? When are we working honestly to support ourselves and our families, and when is it workaholism or greed in order to avoid feeling our feelings?

For ten years, the Himalayan kingdom of Bhutan has used "gross national happiness" to guide national decision-making. They even have an index to measure the collective well-being of their people. I grew up in a poor country. We reused everything. After eating food from a can, we'd keep the can to use for something else—to get water, to store things. We didn't throw anything away. We also shared everything. If I had candy, I would offer some to my classmates.

When I arrived in Holland, I saw a boy eating a chocolate bar all alone. It was my first taste of culture shock. Later I realized it wasn't about Dutch culture, it was about modern economics. People have forgotten the joy of sharing. When everyone has more than enough, sharing gets lost in the shuffle. "If you want some, buy your own." Another time, I needed a drill. I thought everyone on our street had a drill, but I didn't dare ask. I understood by then that you don't ask, you buy your own. One or two drills for the whole neighborhood would have been enough. How often do you need a drill? But economic growth requires that every home have its own. It's crazy.

Economic growth covers over the need to help each other. So many people in the West have enough for themselves and don't see that everything is interconnected. They think they don't need others and that others should shoulder their own burdens, that it's not our co-responsibility to help. Economic growth can mean growing apart, separating ourselves from one another. It seems so obvious, but in fact this is a great disease in our time.

In the past, neighbors, communities, and extended families supported each other, including economically. If your little brother was poor, you'd give him what you could. When he was out of work, you'd help him find a job. And when you were out of work, he'd help you. The same was true of transportation. My father was one of the few people in our family who had a car. Sometimes he would take all the children in the neighborhood on an outing. Without much money, we shared and were happy with what we had. It was more than economics. It was connection.

Sexual Intimacy

A second idea of what will bring us happiness is sex. At its most profound, sex expresses love and intimacy. It's a moment of giving. Real sex needs to go together with real love. If love is not there, sex may become a moment of pride or proving yourself.

In real sex, you don't need to prove yourself. When you love your sexual partner, there will be presence and care. Take time for each other. Nothing will give you more happiness than being together in love, and nothing can separate you faster than sex without love. Sex is a knife with a two-sided blade. It can nourish love or it can nourish desire. Desire always ultimately brings separation and anger. If you love your partner, you'll be less angry. When you give, share, and help, happiness arises spontaneously.

Living together is not always easy. There are a lot of unpleasant times. But you have chosen each other, and that's a profound bond. Sex is more than a romp in the hay. It's an expression of gratitude, even for the pain and suffering. When sex goes hand in hand with love, happiness deepens.

Power

Some people think power will bring them happiness, which often also has to do with money and sex. Donald Trump said, "When you're a star, they let you do it." That is many people's idea of power—the other person has to do what you want. People who value "power over" get angry over the smallest things. People think some things cause happiness and other things cause suffering, but that's not true. The things that bring happiness can also cause suffering. It's about desire and the bandwidth you allow to meet your needs. Are you fixated with a certain object of satisfaction? Does God's gift to you have to take a particular form?

Power is not only toward others but includes your relationship with yourself. Some people are tough on themselves. This is allowed; that is not allowed. We want things to be a certain way. Everything needs to be under control, outside and inside. It simply doesn't work. You increase control, but not your happiness. Growing your project can be the work of a bodhisattva or it can be an act of power as an antidote to feeling impotent. Feeling impotent doesn't go away by creating an empire; it just masks it. In fact, we can't control anything. When power means control, it's doomed. Sooner or later we need to see and feel our low self-esteem, our feeling of impotence and our rage about it.

The alternative is honesty. When we can acknowledge and share the truth of our feelings, our pain, and our suffering, freedom arises naturally. For this to take place, anger can be important. Anger can tell us what we need to see. In a loving relationship, we see each other, warts and all. We don't need to control anyone, least of all ourselves. The gospel of power requires a belief in cause and effect. If we can manipulate the "cause," we can control the "effect." We think we can control everything, make things the way we want.

There is a way to peace. It is love, starting with accepting ourselves with all our flaws and shame. When we can love ourselves, we can care about others, and we're truly peaceful. When you hate yourself, you hate others, and everyone suffers. Do you remember the last time you were happy? Defuse the bomb in your heart. Shine the light of awareness on your anger.

The essence of things is neither good nor bad. We suffer, grow old, and eventually we die. When we get angry, we're full of fire. Our house is on fire. But there is a larger home not limited to our physical body. In every person, we can see a Buddha, an awakening being. We can also see an ordinary, vulnerable person who is weak, angry, desirous, and looking for love and acceptance. To know the truth, we need to see both. There is a Buddha in every ordinary person.

Nourishment

A fourth thing many think can, in itself, bring us happiness is good food. I know foodies who think and talk about gustatory experiences all day long. In the West, we have more food than we need, yet we share less and less. We want to close the borders to migrants, which I hear as "Stay away from my food!" As our basic needs are met, we become less and less hospitable. It's the primal reflex that fuels racism and power politics. We get angry at the people we think are coming to rob our refrigerators, but it's too painful to be honest with ourselves, so we say they're coming to take our jobs. Food is a condition for survival, but even when we have enough, the possibility we might not someday still generates fear and greed.

We can't be happy without sharing. As an antidote to this fear-based greed, you might try reciting these five contemplations before meals:

1. I look at my food and know where it comes from.
2. I see that many people in the world don't have food.
3. I eat this food to give my body proper attention.
4. I know that my mind also needs good nutrition.
5. I will transform this food into insight and compassion.

The first contemplation encourages us to look at our plate of food and know where it comes from. If we look deeply into our food, we see ourselves. We *are* our food. Every day, we eat ourselves. We come from our food, and our food comes from the whole cosmos. Looking into food, we see ourselves and the cosmos. We *are* the cosmos. We are not just separate individuals.

Reciting the second contemplation, we know that many people on earth do not have enough to eat. We are the lucky ones. And we can share what we have with those less fortunate. Sharing, we express gratitude for what we receive, and at the same time, we think about those who need our help and support.

Practicing the third contemplation, we eat carefully to nourish our bodies. When we don't, we can lose our balance and get sick. A lot of modern illness is caused by eating excessively or ingesting non-nutritional foods. We can eat with respect for our bodies and the environment.

It's valuable to learn more about nutrition—which foods feed us and which foods cause heart disease, diabetes, inflammation, and even cancer. The right foods give us the energy to live, to love, and to understand each other.

In the fourth contemplation, we eat carefully to nourish our minds. This is a practice of love. When our mind ingests ideas and images of hatred and anger, it brings about suffering and destruction. When our mind is nourished with love and respect, it produces understanding and fraternity. While eating, carefully watch your mind (and not your smartphone). If you pay attention, you'll see clearly the kinds of food your mind is consuming.

Practicing the fifth contemplation, we transubstantiate what we eat into insight and compassion. Without insight, we can't see the way in daily life. We may fall deeply into loneliness and suffering. We eat in order to live and to show love and support for our fellow travelers on earth. With insight and compassion, we can stop causing suffering to ourselves and to others, and recognize the true happiness we need to live harmoniously together.

Awakening

A fifth idea many people have about what will bring happiness is sleep—a good night's sleep. Sleeping is, of course, an important aspect of well-being. But in some cases, oversleeping can be a message from within that something is amiss and needs attention. Rather than oversleep (sometimes we need to catch up on our sleep) we can ask ourselves, What's wrong? But we in the West also have a thing about people being lazy. Many of us can have all we need without having to work, and instead of celebrating, we berate others.

Like food, there is something of racism in this notion. Let others work for us for next to nothing and we'll enjoy the best food and luxuries without working. (This is an illusion, because greed and fear still make us work harder and harder.) We are rich, but in many ways we are asleep. We think we're smarter, superior, deserving. Feeling superior can be pleasant, but it's a defense masking inner conflicts. We're so accustomed to ease, we can barely handle a little discomfort. When things get difficult, we collapse, so we seek happiness to avoid suffering. Wanting sleep can be a search for insatiable convenience. It keeps us in our comfort zone, while anger brings us out of it.

A life of only pleasant moments doesn't exist. Life always has difficult moments. If you choose only ease and try to avoid difficulties, you'll never find happiness. Difficulties have their place. When children get sick, their immune systems are strengthened. These are periods of growth, and we get strong. It's also true mentally and spiritually. If we can be deeply present during moments of anger and greed, we can learn and become strong. But if we continue pursuing false notions of happiness, we'll stay asleep. The wish to stay asleep is a powerful force. We think it brings us happiness, but it doesn't.

Are you awake? Being awake means experiencing enlightenment. We believe things like money, sex, power, food, and being asleep are causes of happiness, but in fact, they're counterfeit. They're causes of suffering. And when we pursue one, we pursue all five. They're interconnected.

Only when we're truly awake can we look for real

happiness. If we just float downstream, we'll never get stronger. Many things purport to bring happiness that aren't good for us at all. It's tempting to follow these ideas, but they won't bring us happiness.

Co-Happiness

Genuine happiness is deeper than the dualities of joy and suffering. In that sense, genuine happiness is *unattainable*. It only arrives as a *byproduct* of living honestly, connected to oneself. But when it arrives, it's a joy we can share with others. There's more than enough for everyone. The problem is the sense of scarcity. I have X, and you don't. Therein lies the problem. It's the cause of wars as well. I want your oil, your land, your labor. Wars on the battlefield and the wars inside ourselves both come from inside.

To stop wars, stop chasing the causes that purport to bring happiness. We don't share, because we think there will be less happiness for us. In fact, the more we share, the happier we become. Sharing means not grasping, not being consumed by greed, hatred, or delusion, not adhering to the so-called five causes of happiness. If you share your happiness, you'll discover that beneath the grasping and scarcity is a genuine happiness that is stable and, oddly, unattainable. The prerequisite is to stop chasing after it.

I had an aunt in Vietnam who was extremely poor, yet every time we visited her, she always served us mango, papaya, and other delicious dishes. Mangoes in Vietnam are sweet and fragrant, ripened by the sun. And while we were eating her scrumptious food, she watched us with obvious joy. When we asked why she was standing there, not eating, she just smiled. We could feel her happiness.

In true happiness, others are happy and you are too. I'm happy because you are, and in that state, there's no separation between my happiness and your happiness. When we share, the world suddenly becomes beautiful, and we feel grateful for everything we have and everyone we know. We can transubstantiate the five objects by sharing. We give, and awakening arises naturally, because we have no desire to hoard. When we're generous, we're not angry.

Right Attention

The more we give, the happier we become. This is the opposite of what many people believe. Fear, ignorance, and grasping feed the sense of scarcity—there isn't enough for both of us, so I want it. There is a joke that an uber-wealthy person and nine ordinary people are at a table, upon which are ten cookies on a platter. The rich person takes nine of the cookies and tells the others to watch out for the person at the end of the table, because he wants to take their cookie. In the face of such greed, anger, and delusion, within and without, we shut down. We quit trying to find happiness. It's there for the taking and free for everyone, but we can't see it. We can't even imagine it. We're so depressed and angry with ourselves. We can't imagine sharing happiness, it seems in such short supply.

We live in a repetitive dream. Up and down, up and down. We think we're awake, but we're asleep. One day we feel happy, the next day sad. Life passes quickly, like a dream. When we say, "I'm happy," that's not entirely true. When we say, "I'm suffering," that's not entirely true either. These are just categories of mind.

The teacup is *always* empty, even when it is filled with tea. It's the same cup whether filled or empty, because emptiness is its essence. The tea does not *belong* to the cup. Nor is it part of the cup. We are empty too. Always. Even when we're filled with happiness or suffering, we are not that happiness or that suffering. Seeing in this way, we become free from our emotions.

Anger is a product of mind separating the world into categories. When we don't add fuel to a fire, the fire goes out. We don't have to do anything. Laziness has its place. Sometimes doing nothing is an expression of wisdom. We don't feel compelled to do anything.

To do nothing is to let things be, to observe and to act only in the flow of resonant energy, without "doing" anything. If you're a doer and you see a match, you might be afraid of what the match is capable of. But if you're wise, you'll know the nature of the match and you won't do anything. You won't light it unless there's a purpose, and then you'll act with care. This is a way to minimize suffering.

When there is anger, know anger is there and that

you don't have to act on it. It doesn't have to bring about suffering, for you or others. It simply "is," created by your mind dividing things into good and bad, right and wrong, happy and unhappy.

It's a problem when you can't be angry and awake at the same time. You shouldn't have to choose. You can be angry and not act on it, deny it, or repress it. You can *be* with it and remain quiet. Engage your anger in a conversation: "What do you need?" With right attention, you'll know what to do (and what not to do). Perhaps you'll help another person. You can act from wisdom, paying attention to everything, not in a disinterested way, but because you don't *have to* do anything. When you act from stability and awakening, you give respect to life.

Wisdom has no playbook. You just enter a situation and act based on the ingredients in the moment. You are one of those ingredients and so are the people you love. Don't act from the delusion of division. Wisdom is light— illuminating and porous. It's not dense, it floats.

When I was a little boy, at the end of movies the words "The End" appeared on the screen. But "the end" is an illusion. There is no beginning and no ending. Live fully now. Be honest, thoughtful, and compassionate. That is the best advice I can give.

POSTSCRIPT

Until We Meet Again

There is so much violence in the world and in our own minds. When we're in despair, we can't see the beauty of life. But love is possible and it's available to all of us.

The day I completed writing this book, I heard on the news about a massacre in Christchurch, New Zealand. *He shot them when they were praying.* Prayer is an expression of love. When we pray, we are in love. These victims were killed when they were expressing their love through prayer. And the shooter? He was *not* in love. He was in hatred and confusion. He thought there was something righteous in killing. But in killing, there can't be anything righteous. He killed others, and he killed himself—his own life and future. I send my love to all the victims. I know they are all still in love now, still in the loving hearts of everyone. We share the same faith. We believe in love.

I send love to the killer too. I want him to understand that we *can* live together. We cannot hate each other, because deep inside, we *are* each other. We all want to be happy and we all want to be safe. None of us wants to be hurt or killed. No one wants to lose someone they love. No one wants to suffer. You are not different from the men, women, and children you shot. You shot and killed yourself.

I have been consumed by hatred and know how dark it is. The more you hate, the more you turn away from life's light. In New Zealand, we lost fifty uncles and aunts, sisters and brothers. We must work together now so we don't lose any more family members—people, animals, trees, plants, Mother Earth. Our wise friends in New Zealand enacted legislation immediately to try to prevent another slaughter.

Let us say, together, "I don't hate you. I do not want to destroy you or exploit you. No matter where you come from, no matter what you believe in, no matter what you've done, we all forgive, accept, and love you, because you matter. And you are us." Hatred cannot win. Only love can make us whole and bring us together. If we act from the depths of our love, we can overcome all obstacles. Together, in love, we can put an end to greed, hatred, and delusion, and put an end to violence. Love is the way. *Love is the only way to happiness.* Let us discover love in ourselves, then in others, and expand the circle wider and wider until we see love everywhere. Love is already there—we only need to notice.

Until we meet again,
—CUONG LU

ABOUT THE AUTHOR

CUONG LU is a Buddhist teacher ordained by Thich Nhat Hanh at Plum Village. He served as a monk for sixteen years and now teaches in the Netherlands, where he lives with his wife and three children. A former prison chaplain, he is the author of *The Buddha in Jail: Restoring Lives, Finding Hope and Freedom.*

Shambhala Publications is distributed worldwide by Penguin
Random House, Inc., and its subsidiaries.

Library of Congress Cataloging-in-Publication Data
Names: Lu, Cuong, 1968– author.
Title: Wait: a love letter to those in despair / Cuong Lu.
Description: First edition. | Boulder, Colorado:
Shambhala, [2021]
Identifiers: LCCN 2020011081 | ISBN 9781611808803
(hardcover; alk. paper)
Subjects: LCSH: Suffering. | Despair. | Violence—Prevention. |
Suicide—Prevention. | Peace of mind.
Classification: LCC BF789.S8 L82 2021 | DDC 155.9/3—dc23
LC record available at https://lccn.loc.gov/2020011081